London-rose
Beauty Will Save the World

London-rose
Beauty Will Save the World

Fanny Howe

DIVIDED

Published in the United Kingdom by Divided in 2022.

Divided Publishing
Rue de Manchesterstraat 5
1080 Brussels
Belgium

Divided Publishing
Deborah House
Retreat Place
London E9 6RJ
United Kingdom

https://divided.online

Copyright © Fanny Howe, 2022

All rights reserved. No part of this book may be reproduced or transmitted by any means without prior permission of the publisher.

Front cover design by Alex Walker
Cover image from Fanny Howe's *Simone Weil Avenue* (1992), courtesy Fanny Howe
Interior photograph by Jamie Partridge
Printed by PBtisk, Příbram

ISBN 978-1-7398431-1-3

CONTENTS

London-rose   1

Beauty Will Save the World   71

London-rose

Isn't the sky everything to me?

Before 2000 my job was correcting errors others had made. I took cross-country trains every other week to visit young people and administrators to see if their grades were equivalent to grades in the US. Out of date, misread, measured incorrectly; failures of translation, sickness, prejudice—all these indicated that certain standards could not be shared across borders.

During that time, I turned from theology to philosophy and back again to theology. Here I wavered. I was unable to bear too much contradiction but persevered day and night in favoring Scripture and any revelation derived from experience. At the same time the open-endedness of philosophy, where it hovers and suffers, inconsolable with doubts, looked as heroic as poetry.

The students were essentially another migrant population crawling across Earth to find a safe place. A place both recognizable and not. The sky above cleared of anything but satellites, their junk, and war preparations made gray tears fall. If the kids could only re-discover the world inside their retinas. If only they could start over. But their mistakes were written already, and computers under half-developed had absorbed them.

The Irish philosopher of the ninth century Eriugena was said to have been stabbed to death by his students with their pens. Like a wild Gnostic he seemed to think that the world was created by the Serpent, not by God, and stood on the side of the animal and natural world in the war for truth. Or was this just the way I could explain my sympathy for him?

"The end of all motion is its beginning; for it terminates at no other end save its own beginning from which it begins to be moved and to which it tends ever to return, in order to cease and rest in it."

The Serpent was not an architect or warrior but one who lay in wait, watching what went by. He made nothing new but shed the old, returned it to the earth. Eriugena said:
"God running through everything that exists is no different from his act of seeing everything that exists, in fact everything that exists is produced concurrently by God's running and by God's seeing."

He seemed to understand that the world was as strange as it was recognizable.

Like a childless mother I worried over each one of these mysteries along with the students, migrants from the twentieth century. I hid my camera in the bottom of my bag and never turned the lens on them. I wanted to keep our contact free of technology. Their faces born of lands war-torn or ruined didn't need to be identified any more than they were already.

On my first trip outside London a painter and a poet asked me to their house in Wales, among green hills and valleys, a stone house containing books, pictures, dishes, and not one of them American. The local saint is Melangell of the seventeenth century, in whose virgin skirts the hares took refuge when hunted by men. At the head of the Tanat Valley, not far from Llangynog on the main Oswestry road, was where she dwelled, and there now stands a little stone church and graveyard.

The art critic John and I walked through fields away from a massive but thin waterfall, and his large dog was with us, but we lost him, and then a farmer came after us on his moped with two Australian shepherds yelling, spitting, furious because our dog had attacked a ewe. We left with the dog on a rope. Blood spotted its black lips.

The gods pass by as clouds. We see them and look away as if embarrassed by their glories so pathetically begging for notice.

Autumn air, dinner at a big oblong oak table beside a fire. Early darkness. Red flowers on sills. I remember the rough side of American optimism and can't sleep until four a.m.

and then had hideous dreams of being a student again. Rain gets in closed windows.

You move towards someone with confidence, they make one gesture, or say one word, and it makes you falter and you brood on it and never feel the same about the person again. Because of the word or gesture, I wonder, or because of the associations your thought makes with it.

Another walk through the hills, but fog was spangling the greens, and there was the sense of the communalism of the pastoral living which preceded the moving-in of the Anglo-Saxons with their obsession over territory. For so many centuries, there was no boundary in Wales or Ireland, a wandering rather through grasses and rains, and perhaps only the livestock grazing were marked ... Then inside, fire, reading while rain gushed down, the dog snoozed, a cove for happiness.

"It's easier to die than to remember."
To wander without shackles is every god's goal.

From Shrewsbury to London. Gentle country. Clouds like cold white butter, and closer they are silver, opal. They break and multiply, but it's an illusion. They are thinning and thickening according to the number of souls they contain.

Dublin, Cork, Galway, Scotland, Lancaster, Birmingham, Warwick. Trains, rented cars, smelly two-star hotels, and fury at being silenced. No permission to take responsibility for my job. My dread was a sign of building resentment. At the man not allowing me to do my part of the job my own way—taking down information by hand so that I can then enter the information into the computer later and focus my attention on the actual people I am interviewing while they are alive and in front of me. And although the computer program is unevolved and the printer doesn't work, the man is forcing me to enter incomplete information rather than admit that the technology is (wrong) imperfect and it would be better to bring handwritten notes back to the office as I have suggested again and again.

Close view on what's happening in the larger world with office workers. We can identify the failings before they rise to the top. If we tell, we are fired; if we don't tell, we are collaborators.

Devonshire, after a day and night in Diddlington, near Horton and Dorset, with people again. Pumpkin soup. Converse and walk through Hardy's countryside. Question of reversals and inside out. Are we doing our metaphors backwards, or are metaphors reality? Are we on the other side of something, like a thread-back tapestry, our perceptions reversing the experience of the actual? What is missing from everything? Its purpose.

I comment on scenes before my eyes by comparing them to a movie I have seen. The movie comes first.

Slimy silver clouds in the rear-view mirror. View over Lyme Regis to the sea. Maybe everything is mirrored. "Poets are receivers and nothing else." The sky is new in my eyes, but my mind is the same. Depression is irrepressible.

"God can't know God because God doesn't exist." God is all mind and passes with the clouds.

So that explains what I thought I knew already.

Moss grows where light hits. The story of failure asks one question only: what do people who lose do next? "Let the best one win." War is one way. The other way is religion. Let me at the stakes. It's so much a matter of patience. No fury, beyond all reason, no sequence broken, but diverted. Nothing seems to co-operate when you lose control. Blue becomes violet. Bend your head to the blank. The solution is so simple: don't identify yourself with your description of yourself.

Gray and silver mirror each other.

The world wasn't made for the good alone; it may have been made for bullies. The place for purifying sadism. Or maybe it wasn't made at all, has not been made yet, we are told by the Vedas. Thomas Aquinas disapproved of those who confused knowing with believing.

*

Every morning I get up at six and walk the few blocks past a department store, jewelry shops and half-wakened sandwich-makers to get to the office by seven. Then I can work (think) alone on my work before the others arrive. I stay until nearly five when I go to Vespers at Westminster, sung by six big men in the nave devoted to Mary.

A few people come every time with wet bags, battered shoes. There are people sleeping in the shadows and one woman whose whole body is bent as if a branch has shaped her pain, with a sheaf of snow-white hair covering her face. The Byzantine squares shine from candles, and it is the shrine to Saint Joseph that these days I like the best. Joseph the Workman who helped women in trouble.

If poetry could be read as a projection of thought, not as a figure stuck inside thought, it would help assuage its agony.

I have no interest in talking (as my generation has relentlessly boringly, pridefully done) about poetry, poetics, etc. I would rather meditate on disappearance, failure, energy, force, and the persistence of a figure through it all attempting to be both noticed and free. It's almost one of us. The woman gives birth to her own body. It contains the same parts as her own.

Free will and flocking: a perfect arrangement.

These are the important questions to ask: "How do you make money? How do you buy your food? How do you pay your bills? What did you eat today?"
God grant me a bed to sleep in, a roof over my head, a kettle, tea and water, a little fridge, milk, a bun and no one there. Maybe a dog, maybe a fire. A yellow pencil, a legal pad and you.

Nightmares of job failure, paperwork lost, numbers misunderstood. The person who is correcting for a living is impotent. Even if this person can identify the solution to the problem that is creating the errors, she is silenced. A face in front of a screen. Rapt attention. It's no kind of mirror, though a reflection of brainwork passes through fingertip and eye. A locked situation. Mouthless. Filing, checking and comparing numbers. Sending e-mails, faxes, and then the relationships in the office are absolutely based in secrecy. Not so much boundaries as gaps. Creaking stairs. Closed doors. Millions of citizens doing the same.

Doing work for a company that doesn't know your name but recognizes the government number you have been assigned. Even if you can see several ways to make the system function more efficiently, you might as well forget the observations, because sending them out would be a waste of your time. Every—even the most moderate suggestion is erased during utterance. You are a knot in a net, a contributor to some organization that doesn't even know itself. How far from pornography is this kind of body-work?

"The 'dangerous class', [*lumpenproletariat*] the social scum, that passively rotting mass thrown off by the lowest layers of the old society, may, here and there, be swept into the movement by a proletarian revolution; its conditions of life, however, prepare it far more for the part of a bribed tool of reactionary intrigue." (*The Communist Manifesto*). Politicians.

I took the train, then the Hovercraft, and then another train to Paris to see what it felt like. Thanksgiving gray, chilly, a light snow on the fields from Boulogne down—the whiteness of the statues in the Tuileries, the little white roses of Renoir in the Orangerie. I stayed in a hotel near Saint-Julien-le-Pauvre. Walked through the Egyptian adobe of the Louvre, views out into in, and out around the dusk, where flames flew off the carousel and twigs were white.

Stumpy trees with elegant, laced twigs. Walking along the back of benches down an alley of winter trees—a haunting way to meet myself coming the other way. How the objects have acquired layers of association with their repetition through the years, making each sense-experience more poignant, almost unbearably bright, sharp, an unexpected surplus acquired unconsciously by the luck of living so long. Half-gold twigs at evening-tide.

Luck is generally associated with money. Coins are nothing in themselves and only become good through exchange. Therefore, their value is formed in the lack of contact that lies between the coin and the outstretched hand. The imagination.

Paris is better than anywhere yet. It's because of the presence of fulfilled trees and labor everywhere and its integration into the daily working culture. What this does is what religion does: promotes a belief in human potential. We are bent on seeing our way.

Read *Art and Revolution* by John Berger
Read *Beware of Pity* by Stefan Zweig

In London again, twice weekly trekking to the other side of Hampstead Heath to see a psychiatrist, my first time doing such a thing, lying flat in the little white room that feels Dutch, and on the wall a picture of colored ducks, and behind me she sits, a Susan, tall and severe Freudian, but with an attractive melancholy face I only glance at, entering, to guide me out of my bitterness and despair. What if what she believes in is true? What if what I believe in is true? Surely I was trying to come back to reason there.

In winter every object contains an immanent orange, or gold. The word "Broadmoor" carries here a terrible history—criminal madness. Every time I see that word, I stutter. And the Wardour Street sign, hurts. From an earlier life, it has to be to cause such emotional vibrations, War, ward, warden, ardor—or is it a premonition? Are all these words actually amounting to a premonition of something I once knew.

I spoke therapy in the shade of her face: a charmed outdoorsy childhood shaded by the war in Europe. Hatred of grownups. Hatred of school and rules. Hatred of injustice. Breakdown, assassination, grief over father dying, obsessive interest in indifference. To be and to come: experience. Character versus personality is like spirit versus soul, or is it the reverse?

"I don't have that pain anymore."

Many new women (like the therapist) are powerful, chilly, conventional, and their skepticism reaches down deep. Competence, no nonsense, these are their aspirations. I'm scared of them. They are like well-trained soldiers, stiff upper lips included, and the daughters of these women are much the same. The greatest sin in England seems to be the sin of whining. The men unlike the women are nervous, disheveled, but they are good listeners, a trait wholly unknown to American men.

By daybreak, the streets of London are packed with people from everywhere. The city is dirty, gulping pollution from the stuff of cars and buses, and by nine the working people look defeated, in their dark slightly shabby clothes. There is a solid but damp mass in the sky. Nothing blue comes through. Gray, gray. If you look up, though, the architecture is Roman in its territorial weight and claim, it's sublime too, dainty, frivolous, the best the eye has to give. Journalism, literature, self-directed humor, cartooning, lampooning, theater—the British are good at these. And the proletarian feeling of the street-life makes it a city enlarged by the spirit of Marx. But the crumbling feeling around the edges is disturbing, a claustrophobia that creates a pleasing silence in the most public places, a sense of almost Far Eastern formality and secrecy.

Existence is unnecessary, extra. Emptiness is the only necessary element, in order to hold things up, things, that is, that are embellishments. Baudelaire noted this years ago.

On a bus a man takes every chance he can get to look at the woman beside him. Her gaze remains averted. The lover always steals such looks at the beloved. It's how you can tell.

I put on my Walkman at the Victoria bus station and blasted Gregorian chants into my ears. The effect was to make all the people around move to the music, and to take on the appearance of intense spiritual yearning.

"Eyeless ants run after bliss. Legless worms run after bliss. All creatures run, one by one, in the direction of bliss." (Gendün Chöpel)

Lolling hills where sheep are sleeping in the mud, hedges like twine, on the way to Glasgow by train. Topiaries are mysterious creations—wire and twine with vines for skin. Hunters must have invented them. The students are so bursting with terror that they make the mirror crack behind my eyes. The sheep carried languages across borders in their curls—Arabic, Scots.

Someone sustained her sense of control over the world by believing that she had willed her mother to love her sister better than herself, and through the following years she handed away the people she loved to others in order to sustain this first feeling of power. Failure without resentment.

Dream of a bus ride into London, where I get off and meet a handsome man who is about my age, but looks young, he is a derelict. He won't leave me, and I am afraid, but the bus driver who has serene brown skin smiles encouragingly to make me believe I can trust this man. The bus drives away and leaves me in the night with the derelict. My house is not far away and is filled with business and friends. Here I feel safer, but the man, who wants to help, puts my books on shelves and shows this way that he is both educated and eager to move in. I am confused by my hope that it is possible to be a sharer and a loner.

"The zero of hope had yet to be reached." (Thomas Hardy)

I have re-read *Swann's Way*, *The Wings of the Dove*, *The Europeans*, *A Pair of Blue Eyes*, and have plunged through some biographies on the Shelleys. Critical reading: Giorgio Agamben, whose *Coming Community* seems to be hovering at the threshold of revelation. Negative theology, studies in Hinduism, and other material sent from the hermitage in Sonoma. These postcards from the monk I now eagerly wait to see come floating through the wide mail slot in my thick white door. *Nunc aperuit nobis clausa porta.* (Now a door long shut has opened.)

"God took seeds from other worlds and sowed them on Earth, and made his garden grow, and everything that could come up came up, but what grows lives and is alive only through the feeling of its contact with other mysterious worlds; if that feeling grows weak or is destroyed in you, then what has grown up in you will also die. Then you will become indifferent to life and even grow to hate it. That's what I think." (Fyodor Dostoevsky)

In a bed in Lancaster. Little compressed dorm room, after giving a talk called "Democracy" to twelve interns and a man who'd wandered in. Rain and the Lake District outside. Not feeling that well, but better than when traveling with the boss and forced, always forced, until I am literally ill and feel like the inner skin of a cat.

I'm embarrassed by my own letters to others, exposing the bitterness I am feeling. I walk around the flat alone, when it's at its worst, wanting to die. It's as if I had been sipping a poison for the past ten years and it was now beginning to work. It has something to do with my American self as a power-mad machine and even more to do with the natural disappointments of a life now reaching self-judgment. Something to do with family life—my own childhood. And much to do with my work unnoticed (i.e. useless) and the simultaneous success of others close (as close as it is possible to be!) to me in my generation. I am a failure.

Laodicean. In *Anna Karenina* Levin, after his confession and the blessing given by the priest, feels disturbed, empty, vague. He senses that he came near to the truth without wanting to and that it was always there inside him, buried in doubt. I wonder what effect this will have on him later in the novel.

*

All my life I have been obsessed, overly distressed, by injustice, by the way one whole population is turned away at the gates to the palace because of a human preference for force over friendship. I don't progress an inch in my understanding of this phenomenon. It is an indication of evil as a weakness. Four hundred and seventy thousand more years to get out of this degraded era.

At the same time, I refuse to sneer at the people (my parents) who promoted the socialist ideals that came to be flawed. So many people act as if it is they who made the mistake! Most failure is a result of fatigue. Perseverance is one of the greatest virtues.

The office worker relates to her output as a stranger does to her knuckles on a person's door. The gesture is tentative, even slavish. A sheet of paper, a file, some mail. She is alienated not just from the boss and co-workers but from herself on the job because her work goes somewhere invisible and she herself is unlocatable as a messenger. She might as well be an orange in a supermarket. Who judges and cares for her? The person who sucks her juices.

In the academic world the income coming from teaching seems to bear little relationship to the actual time spent in the room. Yet the teachers know when they are there with the students. They can fully experience an exchange of time. Because who, after all, is there doing the job, if it isn't someone who influences the results? But the people working with each other in an office are alienated from their own production because they are only there for the income, and the income bears no relationship to the quality of their time.

There is a pretense in my office that we are doing good work. In reality a digestive disease has taken over this entire system. It runs without purpose, guzzling money at one end and dispensing small amounts at the other. When I suggest a way to cut the diseased section out of the system, no one is there to hear me. All parties recede, notes are unanswered.

Someday human shit will be the only way to diagnose diseases, indulgences and cruelties. The sewer will be the seat of judgment.

The company "is unfit to rule because it is incompetent to assure an existence to its slave within his slavery, because it cannot help letting him sink into such a state that it has to feed him, instead of being fed by him." (*The Communist Manifesto*)

The labor camps must starve the laborers to within an inch of their strength. They exterminate them when they are just about dead.

So far, and probably for decades to come, the way the slave office workers rebel is outside of the workplace. They become hedonists and anti-intellectuals, religious fanatics or reactionary voters. Out of fear, they leap onto the wrong figure of power. They become obese with stagnation. The DNA of fascism so deftly used by the previous generation will show up on stained spoons and feed their children. And more dictators will be born. From the lick of a spoon.

Until the word "slave" is erased from our vocabularies, it will be a marker more terrible than love.

Read Eriugena on Nature

Anything that moves and unfolds is worthy of Earth. Earth is life. Life is made out of dead things. Where does death begin?

Another furious day preparing files to bring along on yet another visit to the interns. I try to explain to the interns, who seem malcontent, that there are people involved in this network of indifference who benefit by taking the apparatus seriously, even though it is absurd. They all agree to see themselves and each other as vital participants—citizens—in an orderly progress. They have determined that only the system can attribute value to their time and they accept the value given without question, because the more they do so, the more they benefit. They accept the system at face value and support it with their crowd. Yet they also have the relaxed neutral good humor of all winners who can vaguely mock their situation. (The doomed ones are the ones who take it all seriously and later question it.)

I tell the interns that often the winners groan over the burdens of working for the system, just enough to ward off feelings of guilt. In this way they can achieve the benefits of being good citizens without breaking a law or experiencing guilt towards the agitated losers. In such a way a reactionary democracy absorbs with tolerant smiles the frenzied outrage of those who question its authority. Losers, by the way, are not rare victims, but represent the majority. Like younger siblings who can't have something because—quite simply—they are lesser. I reassure them by saying there are always more losers than winners.

Never, ever aspire to enter the "middle class," only work to expand it to the breaking point. I concluded my lecture.

Heraclitus said it's natural to know your own mind, be sane. Therefore, actions like war, which drive you insane, are unnatural. The warriors of our time are the least praised. Many go mad or kill themselves.

Sizzle of frost-links between tracks, Anglian, and furred winter clouds. Dawn's grayness shields the fields, a chill burning color from all things. Wool whirled from factory spires, spouts and tunnels in the air. Silk ropes. "The order of the signs" in the Gospels is part of the mystery. B once said that he became a priest in order to live according to a time outside of time, and of course, being a priest, there was no money attached to this time. He was disgusted more by greed than by lust.

We who fear asking for anything because it will show we exist, then learn how to lie and cheat to get what we want and remain invisible.

Sequentia. The sequence contains the secret, and the trick is decoding the sequence, while staying *in* it. It's like looking for the right bridge and the right canal on the Rijk ride through Amsterdam. Or the right letter for the right word in the right sentence that you have never uttered. *Koninklijke pracht in goud en zijde.*

Notes I wrote into my little book for some day:
    Congar on the Holy Spirit
    Allama Iqbal, Pakistani philosopher
    Harry from Hawaii
    Sheila Jordan
    Lennie Tristano, Trotskyite jazzman
    Pierre Jovanovic Inquest on the existence of guardian angels

Walking across the Heath, still, twice weekly, there is often a rain falling that is like a spring rain in New England. There are white blossoms on branches here, in December, tough blossoms almost hawthorn. The Heath itself is like a well-worn carpet, the struggle for grass and leaf to shine anew is a difficult one. The whole of England seems weary. When it's really pouring I stop in a tea-shop and wait. Outside raindrops pulse and gleam on evergreen branches and birds are berserk with pleasure. Behind the cash register are choc-a-logs, snack wafers and signs for orange squash and hot chocolate. Often there are others in the shop with me, mothers with wet-faced children and reading men in dull clothes. The quiet that mutes the occupied spaces in this city continues in this shop. Clink of spoon, splash of tea. Only the shop girls—now called "servers"—whisper together. I generally murmur to the dogs outside who seem to get my jokes.

Galway again, where the moon is setting in the west. Wash the gray into the clouds, and colors into all the rest. The Irish seem to fulfill their entire personalities. I talk to those who are in charge about our interns while they lift a jar and laugh over it, then tell historically accurate stories. Many drunks I have known are two-in-one. Twins in one body, not quite twain. This is true of solitaries too and children who play with dolls.

Galway's early-day darkness, with relentless governing by clouds. The forecast is for sun, showers, heavy rain at times, clear skies, clouds and drizzle. Someone on the radio referred to "the common people of Derry" as being like kids who marry after getting in trouble for an act they didn't commit.

Someone else said the Downing Street Declaration should be treated as a literary document, so that scholars could come and interpret it. She said no one trusts the language of politicians, but they do trust the language of poetry and literature. "Politicians are viewed as despised agents."

They were talking on the radio about Belfast, muttering that children were becoming monsters. Today the solemn novenas begin.

I suppose the English Revolution was the American Revolution.

Cork has natural walls, hills. Round shapes last. Gray stone city, medieval feeling, water rushing through the back of it. I stayed in the Victoria Lodge Inn, one of the few B&Bs so far that was full of light and cleanliness. Here I dreamed, though, that a huge plane careened down and hit a building made of glass that I was inside, I fell with the building but survived, and saw that the ceiling of the next building was made from the belly of the plane which had just crashed. I suppose this means that Ireland would be as good a place as any to die, since coming there gave me my first conversion experience.

Someone said that you have to be a good person to be a good poet. The person said that this was not true of other artists. It was overheard by me. The tree, the bark, the face, the freckles. Arm, ripped t-shirt, a worried look on a nine-year-old face beside the speaker of these words. By now human beings are born with the code of the Law written in: most everyone on the planet knows what living well means.

So in the end (the millennium) the world has been left to us to run. We know the rules, we are on our own. We know what we did to Christ and Saddam and what we do daily again. We know our history of sacrifice and violence has expanded to mass bombing. We must join the plants and animals and destroy the man-made. We know that we are mammals inhabiting a globe that is like another animal and we are eating it up. These wrongs are things we have been taught and we believe because we have seen them.

New scientific equations suggest that there is no difference between past and future, but until I experience that, while knowing it, I won't be able to believe it. For narrative to "work" in poetry or fiction, predictability is a necessity, especially when you are looking back at the work. In other words, predictability is a retroactive activity. Many people struggle all their lives to recreate their first joy. That's one kind of predictability.

"I saw a printing press in Hell." (William Blake)

My printing press will continue to be my camera, and then a projected sentence that asks: *In whose name am I being this thing?*

Many people can't be liberated into their full humanity until their parents die.
"No one now seems to wield sufficient authority to guarantee the truth of an experience, and if they do, it does not in the least occur to them that their own authority has its roots in experience." (Giorgio Agamben)

I hardly ever believe anyone's stories. Instead I think how generous of them to be taking the time to lie to me!

People like me who move from city to city tell the story of our failure. We are seeking something that will make us laugh again and feel at home in any neighborhood. For illegal aliens, contract workers, immigrants, the world remains the soul-making machine, where we are given time to purify the quality of our invisible chemistries on our way home.

The rainbow body is like a puddle full of oil. The mystics who dissolve into it may first have to select the colors they prefer.

*

I saw a movie called *Hors la vie* about the war in Lebanon. It shows villainy with its soft side up. In order to survive I go to two or three movies a week alone and like being there more than anywhere else. I can walk across St. James's Park, along winding paths that crouch under very old deciduous trees and sit with a book in the café at the ICA, stare at people, then hide in the dark with the screen. The anticipation of the lights dimming makes them dim in my eyes before they go down in the house itself.

Such happiness as movies gives me is beyond my ability to describe. The happiness is as sad as saying nobody called.

Transference: the Susan I see on the other side of the Heath has turned into the tall, dark, and handsome female principal at elementary school who terrified me and to whom I believed I must lie in order to deflect her anger. Susan refers to me frequently as an American. I cringe as I enter. She knows I want to die, but I may have to escape from her and my job before I do that. She doesn't understand what dying means (to me).

My eyes have managed to organize the sight of red elderberries among thickly dotted greens so that they form a heart-shaped shrub; this is a memory from early youth. And I can hold it in behind my shut eyes, when I lie flat on her couch, pretending I am on an actual path on a short journey. I am actually a dead body.

I walked alongside a teacher at this northern university. He was spilling energy. He said he was writing a book about cartoons. Political and cultural ones of Jews going back centuries. We stopped under a poplar tree to talk further while university students plowed past.

I noticed in the faces around me a blending of one into the other. There seemed to be little difference between these students physically. Their sameness would make them hard to identify by the FBI. Maybe their appearance was a result of self-preservation. A natural adaptation to the watchful, cruel world.

Roundness was part of the blending, a complacent slope like a soft fur. Chins thick and in many of the men the discovery of a beard's value had spread from face to face, orangey-brown hair coating their chins. The girls were almost all bleach blond, straight-haired, and dull-eyed. What I saw was something like a new breed of human like an apricot poodle. A proud exhibition of toil without duress. Randomness, indifference, giggles without mirth, a secretarial interest in what orders had been given for the day, confidence. Wherever one of them stood out as a failure in conformity, he and she had an aura of solitariness that led them to stand apart. *Solidaire, solitaire.*

These two words to represent a perfect kind of rebel. I stood there thinking that it was true. To be an individual as far as possible, and to share in the fates of our friends, a goal.

Weak rebellions occur every minute as murmured protests and pebbles tossed on water, cleared throats and fingers twisted around each other. To win love—fight a battle.

The dead philosophers of the pre- and post-war period in Europe—they were still my mentors. I could not get past them and their concerns. Could you be both a Communist and struggle for the dignity of a soul, a solitary identity?

Nowhere in the soft faces could I find one suffering, emaciated, yearning, unhealthy rebel. Maybe one girl. Eyes are the hardest part of the human to look at full-on. Eyes are like stones after the rain. There is nothing in them. Balls of water. They shine to signal fear.

The professor's hard face softened into agitation the longer he spoke. He confessed he had to take a trip to Buchenwald and lacked the courage for it. He disgusted himself by his fear. He thought if he went he would make a fool of himself, become distraught, faint, beat someone up. But there was something he had to see.

What is it? I asked.

Nothing.

I would like to see that too, I told him.

I have heard this is the place to see it, or in any of those camps. If only to—life—open: or no love possible.

The last question is God, isn't it?

I was particularly drawn to his hands. Hands are clues to the soul of their owners. Fingernails are supposed to be the endings of the sun's rays. In fact I have studied handwriting, fingerprinting, and the life lines of criminals. On a normal day I would just glance at someone's hands. And then their lips. Both transmit the person's guilt, innocence, sort of, but more the relationship to living things, to humor and disgust.

His fingers seemed to be longer than his palms. They were shapely and light brown. He used them to gesticulate and brush away unpleasantness. They were nervous hands reminding me that nervous systems come from the heart. Or maybe not. I can't remember. But I knew that his circulation was governed by emotions, a tremor, a pulse at his neck.

After his class we met again under a lime tree. I volunteered to travel to Buchenwald with him. I told him I would not bring my camera. He said he would only bring a pad and pencil and he then went and bought our tickets. Two days and a night. I watched his hands and mouth but didn't dare look at his eyes. Eyes are the reflections—no, the collectors—of their possessors' minds. When your eyes lose sight, you still see colors and shadows darting around in the globes, the jelly and retina whirling like the wheels of Ezekiel.

*

Today walking over the Heath I realized that the search for "an audience" is banal since every passer-by is an audience already, and yes the world *is* a stage on which we are performing anyway always. The helpless but pitiless audience that sits apart and at the mercy of the actor is made up of passers-by who have paused and occupy the exact same territory for that time as the actor who is just like them. In other words, the audience and actors are one entwined irruption.

I passed a crowd of children, all of them disabled and mentally unstable, with two teachers who smoked while they watched them. The children's mouths hung open and some of them howled. Their eyes were full of terror as if they were Gnostics recently arrived on Earth, and the spark in each one of them had blown away.

Edith Stein discusses the *geistig* person, the lone self in us who is spirit, who is the portion that is constituted of knowledge. This portion responds as a unified feeling-thing, beyond the psycho-physical creature that accompanies it. This *Geist* is always present to consciousness like a specter.

"The theater and life are the same thing and aren't the same thing. They are made up of the same ingredients, yet the theater wouldn't exist as a form if something different didn't take place." (Peter Brook)

The foundation is emptiness, from that we came, but why?

Don't answer. Who said this?

I, the writer, was responding to my impression of the simultaneity of all existences in the room, and to my understanding of Edith Stein's work on empathy. I agree with the way she sees recognition as lying at the core of human relations.

The idea of audience gives a person the false idea that there is someone bigger than she is who knows more. Greater authority. Even physicists lean towards the concept of participation, as opposed to confrontation. It's not that we are special but that we all are made of something extra.

Gellassenheit: "its first significance is moral. It designates the attitude of a human who no longer regards objects and events according to their usefulness, but who accepts them in their autonomy. This attitude makes them renounce influences, and it produces equanimity. He who has learned how 'to let be' restores all things to their primal freedom; he leaves all things to themselves. He has learned not to subject them to his project but has rid himself of any self-affirmation in which mixed curiosity and acquisition inhibit him." (Meister Eckhart)

Is the pursuit of happiness a religious quest? The self is a clay version of the soul; the self was born the day fieldwork ended. Someone has told me that the self is a bourgeois construct, but we live in the era of this self and therefore are stuck with its tribulations and pleasures. What would Simone Weil say if she saw the world now? Factory work is more productive than ever to the people who never see it, just as unwanted children go into a care system where no one can trace them when they are being hurt.

People walk past workers as if they are plastic statues, leaves, ladders.

Been on the road for days—Hull, Sheffield, here—visiting liaison people, long drives through mottled Yorkshire snowing. One action follows or leads to another, always ending in the smelly cold B&Bs, now in Sheffield, caught in traffic for three hours at night. Over and over again the radio reports the massacre of Palestinians praying in their mosque.

How does the office worker sustain her pretense of interest in the impersonal agency for which she works? The adventure of coffee, lunch, a bit of gossip, pensions? Work all day at a computer and file for a company in which you have no "say"—just for pay—and see how the bitterness finds a way to be expressed.

Every day we stream into the other world and disappear from the day before.

In York the amazing bubbles of color in the Minster's windows—chaos of glass balls. And the whole interior so high and strange like the skeleton of a whale, so much humility lodged in each detail, unnamed laborers whittled at these stones and glass, not expecting a personal audience. Outside black-boned trees, ganglia. Love eludes us just as they say, like a deer or a bird on the wing.

In our father's house are many mansions. If I just knew what I was born for! I recognize nothing. It's all mystery. I have gotten used to the world as it is in the West, but I still don't recognize it. Wood is softer than stone and mechanics have taken down the trees and shrubs. What is all this clatter, buzzing and cutting?

If it's all weird, as in uncanny, it means there is something real, authentic that's hiding or faking. Every statement of fact is an opening for a refutation.

Idihaya means "one who is one." A monk wrote me to say that one of the greatest rewards of growing old is the discovery that there is no duality.

"This dialectical movement which consciousness exercises on itself and which affects both its knowledge and its object, is precisely what is called experience." (Georg Wilhelm Friedrich Hegel)

Motion is where faith starts. 1 Kings 19:7: an angel places a drink and bread at the feet of Elijah who is sleeping and says, "Arise and eat; because the journey is too great for thee."

A story of supernatural kindness.

I followed a small line of people into the bus depot. Red buses, destinations named. Wet sweat in London smells like spaghetti sauce. The buses soak it up and hand it back. I was near the steps inside, hesitated and felt the happiness open doors in moving vehicles can bring.

The professor stood behind me. I felt him before I noticed him. My back was my front. I felt him as if I could see him while I was facing the other way. I didn't dare look while we found our seats, his breath beside me for the long tedious ride to Stansted Airport. While I twisted off my shoes to kick them under the seat, I stole a glance at him and soon we were talking but not face to face. We spoke with our profiles. The bus was warm and comforting. Only small murmurs came from the seats behind. We spoke low in our throats. Who was he? We had made this plan to meet on this day and ride. But he looked different than he did before. All the way back in time. Caricature began in caves. First the bones and bent of animals, then weapons, then humans. Profiles. It was as if full faces were off-limits, too demanding, unless pounded into stone statues.
I asked when a bad drawing becomes a caricature.
I suppose when people become angry at art. Or look too closely at a face.

Hard edges have made civilization ugly. Blocks. A neurotic architecture sees riots, protests, madness, bodies falling, and responds with cement ramps, sealed windows, elevators that go sideways.

"Then we will invent new roses / roses of capitals with petals of squares." (Vladimir Mayakovsky)

The coziness of the bus, its quiet engine, and outside a gray muffler of a sky, our motion—slow—made me think, Please, hope, don't stop! Don't come to an end!

I let myself look at him straight. He was one of those pan-national men with lines and shadows on his skin. He was thin and serious, mouth sensual, eyes lidded and luminous, and his hands he held clasped before him, as if in prayer. I supposed he would be serious in his bones but the laugh lines in his cheeks were not stern. When he turned, his gaze stayed on my mouth rather than my eyes. Our minds were equal, we had nothing to say. It was strange how sure I was that I had not really seen him before. He made perfect sense to me now. Had I mistaken him for someone else? Eyes so bright belong to an artist, a warrior, or a murderer.

*

I felt shame at wishing we were the kind of friends who could touch on a bus, hold hands, lean in and whisper. My cheeks felt hot from the radiator under us. His were a pale red too. Celibacy is not cerebral but blushes like a salamander and intensifies all colors.

Petals of roses, cement squares, we spoke in more depth of why we were going where we were. Don't worry, he said, we are only going to spend one day and one night—in Weimar.

Not in the camp. Ha ha. Those horrors belong to others now, somewhere out in the world.

He dropped his head and literally shuddered with a sharp laugh.

I told him I was flying north to Scotland after this to see more students, This is my job, I explained, my assignment for two years. They put me on a plane from Stansted instead of one from Heathrow.

Death Row.
Row, roses. They open to die. The perfumes are released during transition.

Outside were rows of attached brick houses. People like thieves, walking quickly, not speaking.

Buchenwald must be faced, he said. There is a museum of artifacts there, where I hear there are cartoons. Drawn by prisoners is my guess. Otherwise there are still prison cells and ovens and a room to get washed in. There is a four-acre field with remains of barracks marked. I could see he was afraid.

What's your name?

It was a continuation of the dream I had had of the derelict moving into my house.
I saw the vapors triumph over flesh, a single gesture passing

as an imprint, a Blake. Dreams reveal the insubstantial nature of life itself. If you pulled a dream out of your head, it would be like a veil and tremble before disappearing.

Like seeing a child's drawing of a house with a triangular roof, a fruit tree. Thin pastel lines, all human artifacts with square lines. Familiar.

He was called Warburg. He repeated it and didn't tell me his first name. Warburg reverberated as a little stab in my left temple. What are names telling us?

*

We checked into a cheap tourist hotel, each of us had a small tidy beige room, and set out for the snow-sheeted camp, a morgue that only music could awaken. There was a light snow crisping leaves of grass.

"Happiness without shade, love without limits, a maximum of life without slacking, the most powerful action that is at the same time perfect rest and freedom from all tensions—that is eternal bliss." (Edith Stein)

The struggle for words in the midst of suffering. Why do we need a good vocabulary so badly, especially spoken.

Sheep crossing borders still express themselves in their own birth-tongue—baaa; I wonder why people ring their language into a space where they can keep it safe from contamination by other languages. Borders can't keep voices in, as birds know.

Goethe who sat in the shade at Buchenwald, wrote:
"We do not have to visit a madhouse to find disordered minds; our planet is the mental institution of the universe."

An egotistic poet told me I had made myself a poet through years of labor. Such a gift was not natural to me. Is it ambition or confusion that makes me work on my sentences so hard? What am I looking for when there is nothing there to see?

"They [ikons] are images of holy figures seen in the light of a heaven in which the people believe so as to make the visible world around them *credible.*" (John Berger)

We took a taxi up the hill to the camp. We each nodded off for five minutes, then jumped awake. Each at a different time. Time had lost its beat.
Empty of tourists. Snow was like frost.

Weather a headache on the same side as forgetting. Both sides of my mind work together rarely. Now they do. In Europe—and North America's northeast—there is a series of gray, cold days where the planet seems to have dropped away from the sun towards icy outer space. Night is only a shadow, it's not what it seems to be: a fluid torrent engulfing materials in a suffocating embrace. Night is an immense shadow with an expanding circumference. This shadow opens the lights on the ceiling of our cosmos. They shine and we greet them with our little bulbs. In Russia, in June, sunset and sunrise merge and for a spell it's impossible, all of it.

Buchenwald—snow light on top of a crust of it—sustained a plated meadow. Trees like poles, leafless, but branches begin high up, except for some blackthorn. A misty view over a plateau to low mountains. Entrance long + gloomy along the Road of Blood. One enormous beige building that houses a museum of prisoners' artifacts + upstairs _____. A few rooms—where people were washed—is now a gallery of art done in and after, much of it refined—on yellow parchment with pencil—some paintings—a sculpture gallery—destroyed stuff—photos of prisoners. Under + in back a museum of the Russian (Soviet!) occupation of the camp + the SS held there. The barracks have been "disappeared"—stones mark where they stood—and the infirmary has been re-constructed. The crematorium with baths, doctors' instruments + ovens—all primitive. The hill was high. A brick smokestack—sloping down down through barbed wire. But nothing but MEN in this Buchenwald section—

The smallness of it—
the silence + white
erasure.

How did they work
efficiently?
Didn't! For women they made
satellite work camps
and factories.

What are you?

I forget.
Irish? African?
East?
Jew?
Sorry. I can't.

Fatelessness
An Estate of Memory
A Wall of Two
Night

Looking longingly at the gate, he told me he could go no further. He wanted to go back to town. He had just realized that cartoons in this place could only have been made by the guards, not the prisoners. Why would a prisoner scrawl a series of exaggerated figures of his friends going to the gallows? Was he insane, he wondered. Any cartoon would have to be drawn by a hater.

Here in silence we stopped and turned back and walked down, down, down the hill away from the gate. We never let our fingers touch as if they were sun magnets.

*

You can only be heroic when you have given up hope. "Despair kept him going." (Goethe)—I see that one cannot speak of millions but only of one or two. The feeling that at the heart of a nation is this mechanism that is created by the machines. The thinner your blood was, the more it fought for life, for heat.

*

Patrick Leigh Fermor:
A Time to Keep Silence
a perfect book
Get *A Time of Gifts* by him

Henia Karmel wrote:
"No. Having been taught by machine guns to think in categories of thousands and millions, we had reconciled ourselves to the unimportance of the individual. So did we write in order to transmit the information and thereby incite people later to vengeance? No. In those days we understood the complete futility of trying to match any punishment to this crime."

"We've come too late for the gods to comfort us. They have fled before dying." (unrecorded)

What if the visible world emerges from our minds through our eyes? It was as if children were made of marzipan and butter and were sold as candy.

It would be a mistake.

We separated into our rooms at the hotel. I wrote in my pad to never forget this poem by Mayakovsky. When I wrote it out, I realized it was urging humans to fight against technology.

We will smash the old world
Wildly
we will thunder
a new myth over the world.
We will trample the fence
of time beneath our feet.
We will make a musical scale
of the rainbow.
Roses and dreams
Debased by poets
will unfold
in a new light
for the delight of our eyes
the eyes of big children.
We will invent new roses
roses of capitals with petals of squares.

Room 210, Caledonian Hotel, Edinburgh. Outside the scraped snowy fields of Scotland, and the castle is lighted yellow on the hill outside the window. Heated dressing gowns, a little cold bar, long curtains, delectable beds. This choice, made randomly, suddenly, out of exhaustion after much traveling, was lucky. One night a year this hotel has a deal and offers half-price on rooms in celebration of its anniversary.

Hegel and phenomenology remind some people of Eriugena in his ideas about nature.

White hills over Stirling. Speckled ranges, a fearsome kind of night in a dreary B&B, Eagleton Hotel.

Dreamed of California's coastline houses nested in hills, a hierarchy of houses, and Susan saying to me, with absolute finality, "You did not get the job."

The interns meet me at a bar with a hesitation that makes me think they have heard in advance about my disaffection. Mid-dinner I realize that I am waiting for someone to give me permission to quit. Someone never will. I have to act. But how can I, when I have to make a living? If I don't make a living, and still go on living, I will not be able to work on films. Or live.

Why do I feed the mouth that bites me, and always did?
I roam from house to house like a priest who loves wine and can only find it in the shameless all-night supermarket.

The imperiled ego in mass society: an insect in the chest, struggling belly-up against extermination. Because it is born with the Law built in, the social self creates political correctness for a while in order to avoid killing. Even an insect wants to help its species survive its own violence. Sometimes a butterfly, bright color like pollen, hurries as if a bee might mistake it for a flower, when it is only Death that is chasing it from the moment of its opening into the air.

"Document it." (Edward Said)
One of us must express the problem for the others. Poets should form a political bloc to influence Congress and turn it into pure theater.

And before we exited the bar, I told the interns that they are like invisible angels, here to transcribe what they see and pass it along.

Few ever saw my films about the old woman fishing or the journey of a mother becoming nobody. Unrecognized, undelivered, never found. But guess what? The transcendence in the stories comes with the recognition that there is a language for all this ebullience.

I walk from room to room in the evenings, carrying a space heater to ward off the chill and damp. Listen to music, pray, cry at the most obscure and trivial story. Is this a longing for home, or for life itself? Without my camera, what would I be?

How did I end up this way? A vow I made.
To what? To whom?

I remember addressing myself as if my brain was an x-ray that copied stored words. It had no personality of its own but participated in my breathing and lived in silence. Like a good scribe. Do brains breathe?

*

"Naturalism is unselective: or rather, is selective only in order to present with maximum credibility the immediate scene. It has no basis for selection outside the present; its ideal aim would be to produce a replica, thus preserving the present." (John Berger)

How not to do the above with a camera: "Realism is selective and strives towards the typical. Yet what is typical of a situation is only revealed by its development in relation to other developing situations. Thus realism selects in order to construct a totality ... The medium becomes the palpable model of the artist's ordering consciousness."

Selection, in real life, is lethal. But what he means is not.

In an office the last in the hierarchy is the error-corrector. This person spends her days moving between a file cabinet and a computer. She is dislocated from any actual center. She finds her place at a desk and creates more errors for others even less important to correct. She doesn't do this on purpose, it is inevitable.

Besides in the computer the twigs have lost their buds. Words are dry. They have the "scrupulous indifference" that Bresson ascribes to cameras.

Once I took a weekend trip to Venice on a cheap "Magic of Italy" tour. And on one of those planes that crash. But it didn't. (The airline was called Excalibur). Nearby is the war in Former Yugoslavia which will go on and on. I shot pictures.

Shut façades, pink, brown and green shutters, soft green water, curtains that roll up, black gondolas, sigmoid gargoyles, overcast and orange tiles, Campari and Valpolicella, cuttlefish sauce and Harry's Bar, frosted glass, gelati, dotting leaf as gold leaf of Byzantium, huge green horses and pigeons shitting on Jesus, and drillions of tourists meandering and yawning, wondering how do they carry the sick through these streets and canals. Tourists bordering on hysteria. The yen to transcend. To meander through history. Peace seems more alienating, under these conditions, than war. Eating is the only real experience left for the tourist because food is a body sustaining a body.

Dreamed the shrink spoke through the voice of a Chinese seer named Mr. Yang: "MY letters, MY words, MY sentences."

*

I wrote a practice letter of resignation, explaining my reasons for leaving the job early. But then as usual I was afraid of having no money, no health insurance, no way to live without going to get another detestable job.

Then I walked and filmed. Golden lanterns, lilacs white and blue, neon rhododendrons, bluebells and buttercups, Chalk Farm Road, and somewhere dotted between the lines is the city of London veiled in gray. Long evenings begin their long light. I fear having to stay awake so long, pressured by the sun, alone.

"I wrote to be happy." (Roland Barthes)
To pray without moving your lips is the highest aspiration.

"What if intellectual ambitions were only the imaginary inversions of the failure of temporal ambitions?" (Pierre Bourdieu)

I want to write a list of those people who have not responded to my letters, to let them know that it matters. Most of them are male artists and academics who have become professionalized to the point that they only take time to write their own "work" or letters (e-mails) that in some way feed into their career.

Besides, I have gone away and been forgotten, which is only natural. So I didn't write the list.

In Saxmundham, at the poet W's garden cottage: vegetables first, then a long large part given over to tall flowers, poppies and hollyhocks, where bees were sucking. Slate, orange-tiled, sliding-roof cottage. We walked on a stony beach at Thorpeness, towards a nuclear power plant, then at night we walked through mist and the universal seaside smells, honeysuckle among bitters, mown grass, and we ate trout and she gave me some quotes to think about.

"God and language can be identified, *Dieu* and verb can be the same. What links God, language and woman here is the idea of becoming; God or language is defined in terms of becoming; woman or being in the feminine is also defined in terms of becoming. God and language are both defined in terms of a house or habitation." (Margaret Whitford)

"Autonomy is the true identity of the moral subject, that is to say the true suppression of his alienation." (Jürgen Habermas)

Gray, warm windy Sunday, and I had to call a doctor for medicine. My immune system is listless, as if I've swallowed a vial of opium.
Strangely he gave me lots of sleeping pills knowing that I was suicidal.
Fruitful, and frightful, pain.
Beyond here, words don't go.

I must learn how to turn the double bind into a paradox.

A horrifying observation: "if oppression should disappear, it will have to continue in order to prevent its reappearance." (Simone Weil)

In a pill-saturated dream I was young again and discovered (but don't remember what angel delivered the message) that I am a "great poet" and the proof the angel gave me was that I've been a poet since I was fourteen. I liked the way my years of labor were enough to reassure me of my status. I was being, in a sense, reproached because I should have known it already. But I was happy.

I have to admit, paradox is what repeats and blocks the way forward.

On the bus I see a passage under leaves through mythic villages, a sequence of shadows, and recall one image from *The Wings of the Dove*: Millie on a couch, her head down as if weeping, him leaning over her. His name is Mark and she is telling him that she is dying. Then twenty minutes of water and vapor.

"The entire mass of the weak will have force on its side, while continuing to be weak . . . Number is a force in the hands of him who uses it." (Simone Weil, who knew math and physics well enough)

I dreamed about transparency and mail. Then went for an ultrasound, because my pain was invincible. And some children laughed and played nearby, and I came to life again.

Today a comet a billion times the size of an H-bomb hit Jupiter leaving a hole the size of Earth.

Back to Dublin to instruct the interns, and then to hide away at Lansdowne Park and work. I thought it said London-rose. Solitude, when it becomes too fictional, sitting in a deckchair dunked in plague and fog, no animus, and "I don't know what to do with myself."

The story of the Desert Father Pachomius who asked an angel to let fear become so strong in him that he would be incapable of doing wrong.

"And at once the ray of fear, after the manner of the sun rising on the entire world, and without leaving its place, moved gradually forward toward him. That shining ray was very green and its sight wonderfully terrifying. When fear touched him, it pinched all his members, his heart, his marrow; and his whole body; and at once he fell to the ground and began to writhe like a living fish." (unrecorded)

A transparent green fish, a bardo.

Last night I dreamed I was in my childhood home again, around the house were roses and lilacs, and my parents were there, loving and happy, and I was not a child, but my age now. Then I had a hell dream about my same family robbing me. There was an apartment building, too, which showed parallel lives going on simultaneously.

I took a solitary drive over Ireland and then entered a cave one third of a mile long under the Burren, silver water showers flowed through holes, there were bats and a bear's bones from before history. Tracks from mining, a small crowd of us flowed past phallic stalagmites made of calcite, hard to the touch. Water fills up the cave sometimes and then divers swim through blackness. I was scared out of my wits and claustrophobic because I didn't want to know nothingness.

Outside there was wind over the limestone, walls and walls of stones lifted and leveled for some old purpose all the way to the sea. Foghorns. And around Limerick bright green lilting hills and huge golden trees that swab them. Association between freedom and air continues, even grows, the longer it goes.

Everyone lacks something in their life. The lack is their life. I was born under an eclipse with the many who were also born under one.

Self-pity: a quiet fate. Work all day, nights alone. I don't "count."
When being alone is more than you can stand, bend your head to the pavement. Go to see an Iranian film by the man Lamorisse who made *Le Ballon rouge* and a film about flying over the desert that the West is bombing.

Celibacy's bed: a triangle.
On an Earth, not rotating. Sincerely no.

Bodies That Matter Judith Butler
The Bonds of Love Jessica Benjamin
Hegel's Preface to *The Phenomenology of Spirit*
A Thousand Plateaus Deleuze & Guattari

The body of my work is that child at a distance, that one whose breath I hear sometimes.
It seems that my physical body has been stationary and things passed through it on their way somewhere. The more frequently the same thing passed through, the more of a wound it left behind.

But now I was moving. I left America to come here. Is it better?

I think of willful action as an explosion of content and therefore action is a rupture from form, a shaking-off of form in favor of hope.

I wrote my letter of resignation but didn't mail it. I dread the United States, its speed and sparkle, the high clouds and buildings, its rush of pigeonlike people.

You should never reach out to irony. It should only be a surprise. Irony lights up space like snow in whirling sparks. But it is antithetical to a serious politics.

"The soul takes the middle position between spirit and matter... The spirit does not radiate its essence unconsciously or involuntarily but goes out of itself in personal freedom into its spirit-activity." (Edith Stein)

What we have inherited is pure spirit: an eyeful of planets and stars. O-God has blown away, having implanted science in our cells.

Interns, contract workers, telephone liars and immigrants, modern wanderers, lost at sea, and trampling the Underworld. It is everywhere to be stepped on. Fueled by fossils.

Why is Buddhism more realistic than other religions? If you look into their lessons, their gods, their afterworld, you see it is just as insane as Christianity.

Violently sick in Dingle at the Hotel Skelligs, August 27, on my way to meet foreign students elsewhere.

I spent the first night of this journey in Youghal Motor Inn which was very dirty, overlooking a Travelers' camp. Wandered around the tiny spine of Ballycotton which reminded me of Dalkey Harbor, lovely colored rowboats stacked onto stones and a tiny island afloat on the sea.

Then I drove on to Limerick where a poet served me porridge laced with Irish whiskey which is the reason I am even sicker than before.

Outside the sloping green hills carry shadows in their shoulders. There is a lovely inlet where boats paddle around. Clouds billow, roll. Everything seems right with the world but not with me without my sleeping pills. Ingredients is what we are.

In London I told the boss I wanted to quit. He left the room then advised me to go away instead. "Change your vocabulary back to poetic," the secretary whispered to me. "The corporate world, the health market, they use a very depressing vocabulary. It's almost killing me. It's military." But it's where coincidence takes place, the last gasp of an invisible order.

How do people, so sensitive, so wired to their own hearts, accept the death or disappearance of another person?

In a dream some children save my little dog from being run over, and then my poet friend, the Queen of the Sabbath, says that all she needs to be well is for me to comb her black hair and she will not die. We sit on the steps of my house and I comb her black hair while she drinks a root beer. "The angels of the Lord shall be encamped around those who fear Him."

At Mass the priest said, "God wants us to love the world and stand back from it." How does he know what God wants? I think—if anything—God wants nothing at all. Isn't that the point of God?

"Create expectations in order to fulfill them." (Robert Bresson)

The future comes to meet us from the front, as in walking across the Heath I meet myself at every step approaching the fulfillment of the step.

I don't want to go on seeing Susan for three and a half more months. I feel finished with it. But this is a function of my being a born drop-out. I am like Holy Mother Church who quotes men instead of Herself.

Remember sitting in my office in the corporate building in America and watching the bat-shaped air force planes slamming through the misty skies overhead, practicing for the Gulf War. In fact we were on the edge of Baghdad, there on the Pacific.

Remember too those shiny-suited cyclists—lean and whirring white men, ambitious to the end, driven winners, who have turned the land into a lab. They wear on their bodies the names of companies they work for. How is this kind of naming possible?

My last round of assignments before the new person arrives is here. Bright sun, blue wind, and I have been to Brighton to dine with poets and to Norwich to walk with a friend through a windy New England-like forest.

What do liars want? Images of Germany in the snow on television and a charismatic liar and traitor named Sascha Anderson who worked for the Stasi betraying his friends. It turned out that he was placed in an orphanage as a baby, though he always said that he lived in Weimar until he was fifteen, with his mother and grandparents. The story was about infancy and history and, in the end, outcomes. He had landed on his feet but could not stop lying. People accepted him on those terms. The liar knows that they know he is lying, and he continues in order to humiliate them.

Could anyone love such a liar? Only if they pitied him.

The image of a European park in the winter: wide winding tarmacked lanes, old trees massive and freckled, loops of black steel, ducks in round-ended ponds, and leaves curled in patterns on the green. Then the frost comes. The leaves are moved away. Snow. A silver coating. When the ground seems to rise, the snow comes down to meet it, and statues appear you didn't see before. But it's the time when you walk into an idea that seems to live already in the air. It comes to meet you, enters, then passes by.

Now that I have resigned, I will have no job no matter where I live. I will have no health insurance if I return to America. And I can't live in any other country without a visa.

The same trip as last year begins today.
I lay down sick and couldn't lift my feet to the floor. *Puella, surge*: Get up, girl. Said Jesus to the comatose child.

The day in Paris was warm and sunny, the air soft, the fleshy walls of buildings bent towards each other. Night walk along the Boulevard du Temple. And the next two days were spent in warm misty weather, leaves yellow, shells of chestnuts cracked and flattened, wheat-colored buildings, and nights in the Hotel Unic after long, long walking and filming.

I thought I saw the professor in a café but it wasn't him and I felt my heart tear the way clouds do.

On the way down the hill in Weimar near Buchenwald and after dining without appetite for anything more than alcohol, we stepped outside with our bags.

The word Weimar reminds me of the name Wardour which almost rhymes with Broadmoor. And Warburg.

He realized in those minutes that he was insane to be looking for cartoons and caricatures of Jews in a place created for their extermination. How could he have been so confused?

I said it was the effect of too much thinking about other people's suffering. You can't see pain.

*

The use of one word—"entitled"—to describe the characteristics of the one who gets, and also the one who doesn't get, what each wants. A person who is truly entitled to something is less likely to get it than someone who *believes* she is entitled to it.

In Amsterdam the same slack woman was sitting at the same table. We both drank cognac with rock sugar dropped into it. She hadn't changed a whit, not even her clothes.

"How are the interns?" I asked.

She handed me the notes and said, "The same."

"Will they go on to become productive members of the company?"

"Some. The ones who are most rebellious now."

"They'll get it out of their system?"

"They'll put it into the system. That is, the ones who don't get strangled by psychiatrists, who don't swallow the words schizo and psycho along with their pills."

Did I remember this scene and write it down before, somewhere else? I am pretty sure I did. Why did it matter? Because it had hope in it.

Now in Stirling again, where the sky over Scotland is like a marble in water, sylvan cloud formations, a fat full rainbow and the sharp black shapes of Earth's bones, lambs lower to the ground but closer to heaven. You can drink from the tap here. Birds are busy in the green fall shrubs and berries.

I dreamed I went to the Carmel Valley, saw it from Torrey Pines down to the marshes and salt lagoons where white birds were like the thick smidgeons of paint on eighteenth-century canvases, and there was the cluster of houses where I lived before the vine turned. There! I thought. Maybe I should go back and lie down there.

I dreamed I was a disciple of Ramakrishna's on the ashram veranda. I was "near the end" but not unhappy and surrounded by vivid East Asian women.

Luminous over Galway, pale pinks and blues and the rushing Corrib over stones bluing on the battlements. A man was jerking off on a wall. After work (done, finally, in my own fashion) and meeting with the staff I walked again through Galway town, slate gray, to Kenny's Bookshop to buy children's books, and I visited Nora Barnacle's tiny house, seven children stuffed inside, and walked with a woman named Sheila who explained problems the Irish have with the European Commission.

Cork again, then home to London, and on with the treks across Hampstead Heath. And the surrounding transparency, including myself, increases as my escape from this pattern approaches.

"Psychoanalysis can manifest to the religious man a caricature of himself, but it leaves him the duty of meditating on the possibility of not resembling this hideous double." (Paul Ricœur)

Ramakrishna tells the story of a doll carved out of a block of salt that is dropped into the salt sea in order to measure the depth of the sea, and the little doll dissolves on its way down, and this, says Ramakrishna, is how ecstasy is experienced. I know that Susan sees me as an American innocent. But strangely the fundamental disagreements between us do nothing to stop me from continuing. They almost act as a goad. I actually believe what Ramakrishna said.

I think my problem from childhood has been my longing for a system to explain the world to me. It would have been better to study human behavior and foibles. Instead, I wanted to know what everything meant. In one word.

I continue to work on editing my film in the office, whenever I can grab a moment, because this is all I care about doing before I leave. Each scene is a poem.

Then I had to head north again, back to York, by train to work, and the air is already wintery up here and I can't sleep for thinking about my amateur film.

Yorkshire's land seems like a rolled-out textile, flat and thick. I think about Charlotte Brontë's unborn baby's lace cap. Then speed on to Leeds, wondering if a person can visualize geological structures in three dimensions from on top of the Earth.

Leeds reminded me of America, cement gloom that stuck to the windowpanes. Laboratory rats, now students, who just want to be left alone with their equipment.

A bomb went off in Tel Aviv, killing many Jews on a bus. And I dreamed about Hitler, being in a kitchen with him, and he was young and square like a building. He smelled of piss.

An ontology of grayness. World War Two is forever gray as a fingerprint on my brain.

Many sentences are in the past tense because in fact what they describe will never happen again.
The past tense is the equivalent of the river Lethe where the water doesn't move until moved.
How to explain direction, distance, disappearance.
The triumph of the present tense. Declarative, shadowless.
Often powerful people live only in the present tense. Weaker people congregate to call down the glorious wind for help. God is outside time and tense, always moving. If God is dead, even the name, we are dead too. It's only in relation to God that humans exist.

Some experience is pre, some is post. The epiphany occurs as a slip out of all experience. Déjà vu resembles epiphany as does a shocking coincidence. Something slides out of place and overlaps onto the present moment.
Revelation can be sudden and ordinary: "He doesn't love me." "But maybe he does." (Simone Weil)

The wandering became tedious in time, the hotels drab and thickened by the breath of past residents, the desperate effort to plan the route ahead, then the anxiety when it looked so useless, a waste of time, without the work I loved spread out before me.

Why live?
What do I love?
Is weather nature?
Is work?

*

Where I could end up, year after year, for a spell of safety, was in a monastery guesthouse on the edge of Tipperary, with the order of the days and the hours marked out. There I could fully exist without fear, walk in moist forests among birdsong, bells and bees.
I could do this because there was nowhere else to go once you were there. It was "a final resting place."
It wasn't school. I was not being judged (noted). I was at last truly invisible the way I always seemed to want myself to be. Transparent, air in motion, rhythmic sun and shadow, the way a bird can be.

Animals with their patterned coats, birds with their feathers: able to be fully alive because of their reproduction, uniformity and speed. They were the blessed ones, even the ants and worms, the unwinding snake with its lips in the dirt.

(A mother sheds her skin when she gives birth. She is empty and discarded until the infant can suckle on her nipple. She is empty on the sheets. Blood and a blue umbilicus.)
She now knows what it is to be nobody.

Ma, did I make a choice to leave my job and be poor again? Did I make a choice to return to America? Did I make a choice to live or to die? I don't remember any of my choices outside of those I made in editing video.

There were so many contingencies and so much beauty. The function of the image: what is it? Not to transcend, but to see things as they are. Still an underworld exists in each individual.

Now I am in Sheffield, then I am in Hull, whose austere stone houses lead only to the sea and the Humberside Bridge that looks like the Bay Bridge in the middle of nowhere. Red beech leaves dangle at the B&B window. The Larkin Building is where I sit and wait to begin work, and watch men pushing barrels around, while they pick up leaves. There are still flowers in color up in this part of the world, and Holland is not far away, the way it usually is, for me.

Now I am in the George Hotel in Colchester after a day's work. The weather yesterday was wild: post-rain-puddle-blown-clear-winded-blue-aired. Felt like Boston in early winter. In this room there are black Tudor beams, sagging white ceilings, and a paste-like wall. Again, red beech leaves are swaying against the window. That red reminds me of something I lost in America.

If I go back I must learn how to spit out the poison before swallowing it.
I must go everywhere with children or a dog.

An American woman at my goodbye party bit into a quail's egg and said, "I hate nature."

I don't know why I am leaving or where I am going but I am joining a surge of unmoored people, of contract workers, manual laborers, skilled white-collar workers and thinkers awkward with their fingers.

Who told us to do what?

Where are our politics? Why did we leave? Can this march become a revolution? For what? If it is just for some sky to breathe, a sip of river water, would it be karma that could explain this to us? It is certain to us all that we cannot live on bread alone. Religious ideas are flaming out of our heads alongside the dim fuel of social change. One of them will catch. It will be a borderless revolution, anti-nationalist, a revolution based on an emotion, not an imperialist idea. Music must take care of the children.
Resistance, abolition, eternity!

I never got to film the silver flowers of a moon garden that my friend told me about.

It's as if I had rowed a boat alone across a night ocean. All the above has a grayness to it, like a ghost "who fills the universe in all its parts."

Beauty Will Save the World

Start date: 15/2/1985

WISHES:

To participate in evolution as an aesthetic adventure by using limited materials (those supplied from the past) in a process which had no known goal. Mutations would occur from the coupling of words which were opposite but equal, and separate but the same.

By combining chance with deliberate choice, I wanted to suffer embarrassment on the page.

If the senses are tentacles, then my own motion through a forest of words would be an imitation of that rooting around.

INFLUENCES:

Time, courage and a course called Introduction to Spirituality which concentrated on the Gospel of John. My entire desire at that time was to become enlightened by language and liturgy. Liberation theology was my usual way of remaining grounded in the ways of the world. I hadn't used the techniques of my generation (appropriation, intertextuality) but was not far from their thinking when it came to politics in the secular city.

The course was led by a priest, a troubled person who needed the ravings of a mystic to keep him alive. It was ugly February weather outside. He made some female students angry, and the rulers of the school where he taught were also angry, because he let in anyone who wanted to attend.

These poems come from that time.

METHOD:

I invented some rules for myself so I could press order into the vast untamed thinking in John. I wanted to see if a thought was made of individual sentences or of single words.

Recapitulation. To rewrite. To move certain words from one place to another to see how this altered the trajectory of the poem. To see how resistant a word is to a new thought, and vice versa. To test my ability to think in a new vocabulary and take a new path into the world.

It was almost a science. A real experiment.

Funnily I don't want to say if it succeeded in bringing me nearer to my "entire desire." But it brought me pleasure because it rocked and spilled and tore up. Enough.

I wasn't just a memory but a lot
Like one you forget
When you're not afraid. Take the space
I leave, it's not mine. I am a place for you
To see far to: a vase, a threshold
Entering a floor of earth
Moisture meaning sorrow
My home was only overcome by an estimate
And step. No door you could flee for
Inhaling I'm free

Fountains fall like umbrellas
There is always snow on somebody
Far away. Like youth in heaven
Or a spirit too big a minute
Disappears and cinders since creation
Multiply and close
For the way is by somebody gone
After a year or a day when nobody
Looks back, small spirits
File up

Sometimes the job gets you and sometimes
You get the job. Jupiter, winking star:
Physical knowledge is always off far
And God the utter stranger
Now a creature is free now equal
This is our history, vulnerable but grateful
And thirty percent chance of showers
For the unclean thing held to be holy
The factor intrinsic to illumination
Is knowing that there is no inner light

Jesus argues for those lost
And born above politics
So out of reach of those who value logic
Raise our hearts, Mother, and love
Until they're magic. The brothers
Will argue that Father used to harden
His realism until he was found hiding
Among sisters there's a name for oppression
On the last day till now
But the lips won't speak with consensus

The brown recluse wears a violin design
No dolls but a prayer wheel. It's a spider
Who trusts the fall like an expert
This is a very old child's story
Absolute otherness gives the weight to gravity
Before the job was complete the Lord paid us
Work's never been as good again
Pass. All pass. The North cashed the ice in
And seven days of solid mist
Lay in which to plan well and lose the gist

Some hand got the jet to fly
Above the cold front on Buzzard's Bay
So participation in the Incarnation is hidden
Inside the wet and the red
And a description of perfection
Is too good to bear when the root of patience
Is suffering. It's a risk to be glad
In company eating wine with bread
Every human thought and weakness is exposed
In a smile till joy looks tragic

Where the bread of heaven feeds the air
Inside my mouth, it's home, not that wall
The jail I'm in must be exile
It's horrible, misunderstanding
One out of every seven who leaves bed is good
So where is this place
That starts with a night, then breaks
Into clouds which burn, fall and me wake
To be ignorant—which is one thing—
To choose to be ignorant, another, a sin

Sometimes a stranger has no inner life
But the factor of being this vulnerable
Gets her a history
And a job open to illumination
And sometimes this job is held
To be holy, intrinsic to knowing
Thirty unclean things are winking off far
Grateful as showers and chance
For knowledge is free
To creatures utterly physical

As mermaids who plan to let go
With a splash of stars
And stay in contact with the dark
Through a glaze
On their mirrors you can recognize
Your ideas and tame them
Your space is then a hard old dance floor
Like a piece of chalk
You're allotted some expertise
By showing your eyes off

Children who retreat inside the trees
Faster than any hesitant speech
See their broken brothers spend their perfection
In actions which stink of greed
Each one has a dollar for every idea
To better their livestock
For a few quarters. In every exchange
Of living for playing
They never look better than their branches
Say the bold children

The black telephone circulates
A stimulating universe
Through the hole I report my answer
Which draws long panic inside
Red morality
Don't tie me up
In tunnel tones but merriment
Like cognac lift up my spirits
So they'll stop annoying
The guard of the ordinary

Ruby shoes are rushing by the wilderness
Which makes all parties turn their heads
Up above Mars and Saturn are the Sabbath stars
A woman hunts around for happiness she'll never get
It was a mistake to find out
Now mushrooms in the soil of Caesar
Look like penises and half-girls
So layers of wet thunder belt across the woods
Where the rain unravels the ivy unable
To recover these great interpretations

Half-thunder on the Sabbath
Makes shoes turn in the soil
For mistakes are like ways
You hunt stars out
In the wilderness but can never get
That rush of happiness where ivy's unable
To unravel itself. By now
Saturn's belt is ruby-wet
And rain brings a rush of interpretation
To parties heading away from the woods

A worm rides between walls
There's no getting back to color
Humanity gives two leaps
And the air jiggles like hell
If people want to be innocent
Rain will unfasten some sweets
And you now may enter solitude
Radiant as roses
In their atomic energy
Pressed between emotions

A smile under a hand is still red
In the perfection of thought
A jet of descriptions
Makes you tragic
Too good for company
Fly inside and the risk of joy
Can't be exposed but eat
In suffering and patience
Will root you in your bread
Cold—unblessed

In the Fall from sin to home
Air might start with a mouth
Like a horrible jail
And night burn down the seven walls
Where the bread of exile
Kept us and fed us
Good and misunderstood
But if, and when, we are placed
In clouds, we might at last
Wake heaven to our cause

An expert has never been at work
But trust in which the wheel was planned
Again and brown spiders, solid violins
And dolls designed
For cash by some absolute recluse
While seven lay planning in mist
It was the fall and gravity's ice weighed in
And in The Story of the North an old child
Prays that good will wear
And all will be complete

A third cardinal scandal
Is when we each stand red in the faith
That the world's dread
Will tell only half the story. Acorn trees
And aptitude tests scatter the facts:
Some passed by too many people
And failed to love droves of needfuls
Because they didn't give
A tinker's damn for the others
The rest of us fevered from hope

I will never run to I AM
For advice of a moral nature but blind
Myself for history where little hearts
Talk socialist day and night
Lead me not into cowardly lines
There the people speak with finesse:
"Don't worry, you deserve it."
No, God hardly ever intervenes but exists
As an abiding causality while the broken creature
Is alone so! alone with its errors

Heads are bowed in the seedy old Court
Each aching from shadows half as strange
As the creator. Is that my life
Such a hardship, too, spending all our days
In the judiciary making connections
Look new and tricks for a penalty or sin
In us they say God's been testing out creation
Then escapes at Resurrection
He disappears without paying every time
Said a woman to a man

Tell me what is ordinary
And let me hear the way to kindness and be merry
Guards circulate inside the tunnels
Of our moral universe
Reporting traffic tie-ups by telephone
I can't even lift up to answer
Because annoying tones in my mind won't rest
In this long black sun-chasing hole
With a spirit as red as cognac
I'm drawing on the stimulant of panic

A worm of energy in radiant skin
Aspires to humanity entering today
From the rain to the sublime
In one sweet leap. You ride the sky
While jiggling roses come unfastened
Great solitude reveals how flesh is pressed
Between two walls of air, emotions
Make hell for the innocent
No I want to get back to people and things
To the plus of colored atoms

You've been gone one minute and already
Your spirit is back. What I file away multiplies
While heaven is the uppermost part of creation
Cinder-like snow falls on umbrellas
There is nobody as close as somebody
Utterly gone. Take Ponce de León
Since the ninety-eighth day of that year
He looked for the fountain of youth
You are always in the way of yourself
Too old, or small, until you or your dream disappears

PERPLEXITIES:

Beginning lies at a great distance, and the poor are closest to this beginning, along with others who stand aside.
Freedom is synonymous with less, not more.

What is distant gives the appearance of perfection as it also creates sorrow in the witness.

Do birds and beasts still think they live in Eden?
Do all of us carry the knowledge of the primordial in our skin and bones?
If so, it must be beautiful.

God appears in darkness, the sacraments in light.

When you see someone coming out of a crowd, and you recognize them, why do you feel such—

God's will is not present in technology or in its effects. All those things belong to humanity: this is the horror of the twentieth century.

Many thanks to Camilla, Eleanor and Jacob at Divided Publishing in the UK, and to Chris, Hedi and Janique at Semiotext(e) in the US, 2022.

And to Khushal Gujadhur, the poet, who scanned in Santa Cruz, 2021.

A version of *Beauty Will Save the World* was previously published by The Figures in Great Barrington, Massachusetts in 1985 as *Introduction to the World*.

Fanny Howe (1940–2025) was the author of more than fifty books of poetry and prose. She taught literature and writing throughout her life and was professor emerita in literature at the University of California, San Diego. Howe mentored a generation of American poets, activists and scholars working at the intersection of experimental and metaphysical forms of thinking.